A New True Book

FOSSILS

By Allan Roberts

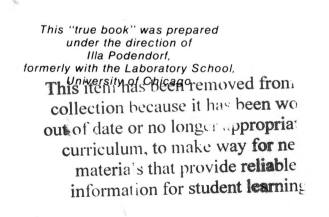

*This "true book" was prepared
under the direction of
Illa Podendorf,
formerly with the Laboratory School,
University of Chicago*

ℚ CHILDRENS PRESS, CHICAGO

Plant fossil (Annularia stellata)

PHOTO CREDITS

Root Resources: ©Louise K. Broman—cover, 2, 8
(2 photos), 10 (2 photos), 34 (2 photos), 43 (right)

Allan Roberts—6 (2 photos), 13 (2 photos), 15, 16, 19
(2 photos), 21 (2 photos), 27 (left), 28, 30, 33
(2 photos), 36, 38 (2 photos), 42, 44 (top and bottom
right)

Lynn M. Stone—4 (top), 40, 44 (bottom right)

Joseph A. DiChello, Jr.—41

James P. Rowan—29

Kitty Kohout—43 (bottom left)

Connecticut Department of Economic Development—
4 (bottom)

Reinhard Brucker—18 (2 photos), 24, 43 (top left)

Field Museum of Natural History—23, 32

Smithsonian Institution: National Museum of Natural
History—27 (right)

COVER—Forty-million-year-old fossil fish found in
Green River, Wyoming

Library of Congress Cataloging in Publication Data

Roberts, Allan.
  Fossils.

  (A New true book)
  Includes index.
  Summary: Explains how the remains of an animal or
plant fossilize over millions of years, where fossils
may be found, and what we can learn from them.
  1. Paleontology—Juvenile literature.
[1. Paleontology.   2.   Fossils]   I.   Title.
QE714.5.R58   1983   560   82-23521
ISBN 0-516-01678-4   AACR2

TABLE OF CONTENTS

Two fossils: tree bark (left), leaf (right)

Dinosaur footprints in Connecticut

WHAT IS A FOSSIL?

A fossil is the remains of an animal or plant. A fossil can be thousands or millions of years old!

Fossils can be bones. They can also be tracks, tunnels, or other "signs" left by ancient life.

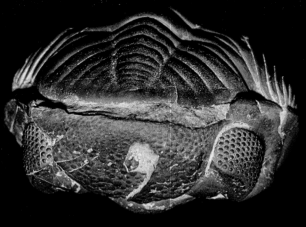

Above: Front view of trilobite
(TRY • low • byte) showing compound eyes.
Right: Close-up of the skull of a flesh-
eating dinosaur, Gorgosaurus
(gor • guh • SORE • us), that lived
75 million years ago.

Fossils tell us what life
was like on earth long
ago.

The study of fossils is
called paleontology.

WHAT HAPPENS TO DEAD ANIMALS AND PLANTS?

All animals and plants die.

After dying, animals and plants are first eaten by "scavengers." Vultures, turtles, crabs, and insects eat dead animals. They are scavengers. Insects eating dead wood are also scavengers.

These scavengers often will eat the complete animal or plant.

Even if scavengers do not eat the dead animal or plant, it will usually still disappear completely because of "decay."

Decay is caused by bacteria. The bacteria break down the plant or animal tissues into chemicals. These chemicals then return to the soil or water.

Above: Insect fossil
Left: Seed fern fossil

No fossils can be formed if all the remains are eaten by scavengers or destroyed by bacteria.

9

Millipede (MIL • ih • peed) fossil

Crab fossil found in sandstone

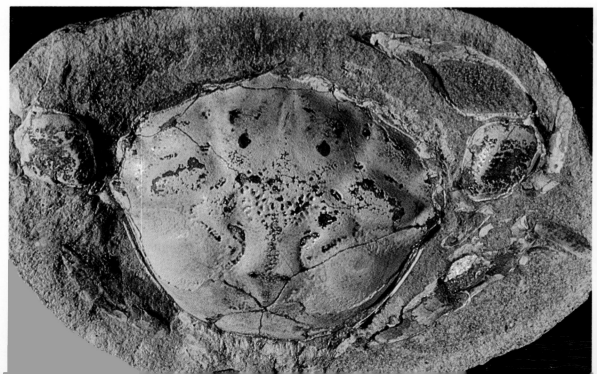

HOW ARE FOSSILS FORMED?

Fossils can be formed in many ways. Sometimes mud or sand covers the dead animal or plant. When the "soft" parts of the animal or plant decay, the mud or sand will fill in the empty "spaces."

Hard parts, such as shells, bone, or wood, will sometimes not decay. They will stay in the mud. Over a long period of time, the mud might turn into rock.

Shale is a rock that used to be mud. Sandstone is a rock that used to be sand. Many fossils have been found in both these types of rock.

Left: Sandstone is a
      sedimentary rock.
Above: Slate is a metamorphic
      rock formed from
      sedimentary rocks,
      such as shales.

Rocks made from mud
or sand are called
sedimentary rocks. Most
fossils are found in
sedimentary rocks.

PETRIFIED FOSSILS

Some fossils, or remains, are turned into stone. This happens when bone or wood is covered with wet mud and sand. In time, water slowly dissolves the chemicals in the bone or wood cells.

These old chemicals are slowly replaced with other chemicals. Over a long period of time the bone or wood is completely

Petrified wood has been changed to stone.

changed into stone.
   Petrified fossils of
dinosaur bones and wood
have been found.

Dinosaur bones uncovered in the Morrison formation in
Dinosaur National Monument

In Dinosaur National Monument you can watch scientists digging up petrified fossils.

This place once was a bend in an ancient river. As the animals died, their bones were covered with wet sand. In time their bones were petrified.

Above: Dimetrodon (DY • metra • don)
skeleton
Right: Skeleton of Tyranosaurus Rex
(ty • ran • ah • SORE • us REX)

Many of these bones
have been put together.
Today complete dinosaur
skeletons can be seen in
many museums!

Bones of small horses,
hogs, camels, and even
rhinos have been found at

Above: Turtle shell fossil from Badlands
National Park
Left: Petrified wood from the
Petrified Forest National Park

Badlands National Park in South Dakota. Even entire petrified turtle shells have been uncovered.

If you wish to see beautiful fossil trees, visit Petrified Forest National Park in Arizona.

FOSSILS IN AMBER

Amber is hardened resin. Resin is the "juice" inside evergreen trees. Today we use the resin of pine trees to make turpentine.

Whenever trees are injured, resin oozes out. Resin is sticky. Many insects, spiders, and millipedes are trapped by this resin.

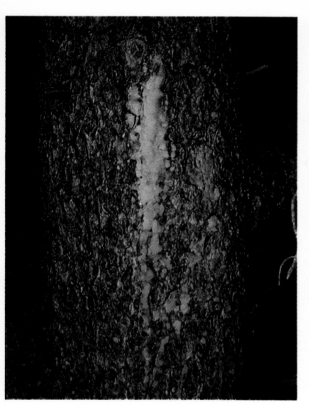

Left: Resin oozing out of modern
       pine tree
Above: Ant trapped in amber
        millions of years ago

Millions of years ago animals were trapped in resin. They did not decay. In time the resin became hard and turned into amber.

Some of these fossils have been found in amber. Each hair, eye, and leg of the insect has been perfectly preserved.

This process of making fossils is still taking place today. Just think, the insects caught in resin today might become some of the fossils of the future.

FOSSILS IN ICE

The bodies of woolly mammoths have been uncovered in the icy frozen ground of Alaska and Siberia.

Ice Age in Europe showing woolly mammoths and rhinoceroses

The Eskimos used to feed the meat of these frozen fossils to their dogs. At one time nearly half of the world's supply of ivory came from the tusks of fossil mammoths.

Skeleton of woolly mammoth

The frozen blood vessels, muscles, hair, skin, stomachs, and other body organs of these mammoths have been preserved and studied.

Some of these mammoths are in museums. In order to keep them frozen, they are put in large freezers with glass fronts.

FOSSILS IN TAR

Fossils have been found in tar pits.

In some places, natural tar oozes up out of the ground and even forms pools of tar.

Since water can also be found in these places, the animals once probably came here to drink.

Some were trapped in the sticky tar. Many died there. The bones of ground

Fossils of extinct elephants and saber-toothed cats have been found at LaBrea Tar Pits in California. Models have been put in tar pits to show visitors how these prehistoric creatures were trapped in tar.

sloths, mammoths, saber-toothed tigers, bears, antelope, camels, geese, and eagles have been found in tar pits. Large insects fossilized in tar have also been discovered.

27

**Fossilized
sweetgum leaf**

FOSSILS OF CARBON

All living animals and
plants have carbon in their
bodies. When some plants
and fish were turned into
fossils, this carbon was left
in the rocks. A perfect

Fossil fish

imprint of a leaf or fish in
rock might also be "black"
in color. This black color is
what is left of the carbon
that the animal or plant
had inside of it while living
long ago.

Dinosaur tracks in sandstone. The hand of a three-year-old Indian girl is shown to demonstrate size.

OTHER INTERESTING FOSSILS

If a crab, bird, or dinosaur walked across soft mud or sand, it sometimes left its footprints. A few of these footprints are now preserved in stone. This is because the mud or sand was later turned into rock.

Thousands of insects live in dead wood today. Other insects did the same thing millions of years ago.

Thousands of pieces of petrified wood have been found that show the tunnels made by ancient insects. Of course, these tunnels were made before the wood was petrified.

Protoceratops was a dinosaur about five to six feet long. It used to lay eggs in the sand, as turtles do today.

Some of these eggs were found fossilized from 75 million years ago.

Protoceratops (pro • toh • SAIR • ah • tops) display at the Field Museum of Natural History in Chicago

Close-up of the skull of a Protoceratops
(left) and its fossilized eggs (above)

Scientists have opened
some of these "rock eggs."
To their surprise they
discovered some of the
eggs contained the
petrified bones of unborn
baby dinosaurs.

Using geological hammers scientists uncovered the
annularia (ann • uh • LAIR • ee • ya) plant fossil shown below.

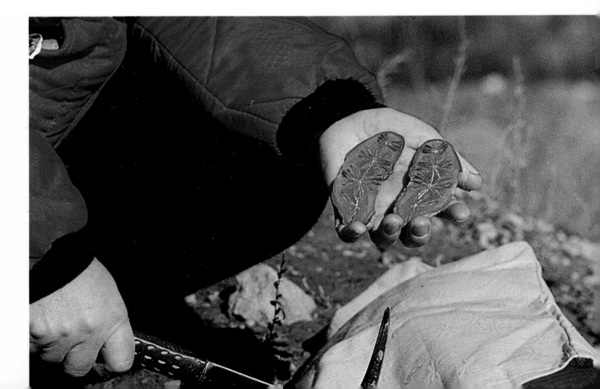

COLLECTING FOSSILS

Many governments have laws to stop people from digging up rare fossils, such as dinosaurs. They let only scientists dig for them because they know how to correctly remove the bones.

However, there are millions of common fossils in the earth. Many of them you can collect.

Above: Buttermilk Falls in New York State
Right: Snake River in Grand Teton
National Park

The best place to look for fossils are where different "layers" of rock can be seen.

Look where roads cut through hills and mountains. Look along stream beds.

Always take an adult along with you. Also, ask permission from the owner of the land before looking for fossils. Many times the owner, or other local people, will show you the best places to look.

Be careful. Rock ledges might break, causing you to fall.

You can also find fossils at "fossil and rock shows." It is here that people gather to sell and trade their fossil "finds."

Tree ferns (above) are living fossils. Fossils of tree ferns have been found dating from the Coal Age in prehistoric times (below).

FOSSILS ARE IMPORTANT

Fossils are important.
Have you ever heard anyone talk about "fossil fuel?" Gas, coal, and oil are fossil fuels. They have been made by fossil deposits of plants and animals!

We need fossil fuels. We heat our buildings and homes with them. They are used to run our buses, cars, trains, ships, and airplanes, too.

We use fossils to show us where to drill for the oil and gas we need.

Many buildings are made of stone. Limestone is a

Shells in limestone

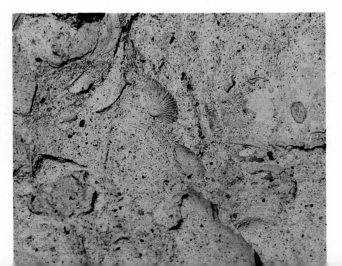

The Rare-book Library at Yale University has marble panels.
Marble is made from limestone.

Sea life as it was about 400 million years ago.

rock formed by the remains of ancient animals and plants of the oceans.

Even the chalk that you use at school is made from the remains of tiny fossils.

Some of the prettiest
scenery in the world is the
result of rocks formed by
dead animals and plants.

Above right: Fossil shells
Top left: Petrified wood
Left: Plant fossil

Above: Model of a fossil dragonfly that lived during the Coal Age. The wings of this prehistoric dragonfly were two-and-a-half feet across.
Right: Model of archaeopteryx (are • kay • OP • ter • ix), the first bird.
Below: Student examines a fossil.

Every fossil can tell us a story of past life as it used to be. Without fossil deposits, we would know very little about the plants and animals that lived millions of years ago. Our knowledge of the history of the earth would be incomplete.

WORDS YOU SHOULD KNOW

ancient (AIN • shent) —of times long ago

carbon (KAR • bun) —a chemical element found in all living things

decay (dee • KAY) —to rot

embryo (EM • bree • oh) —a plant or animal when it is just beginning to develop from a seed or egg

extinct (ex • TINKT) —no longer existing; died out

gully (GULL • ee) —a ditch cut in the earth by flowing water

fossil (FAWSS • ill) —the remains or traces of a plant or animal that lived long ago

imprint (IM • print) —a mark, pattern, or design made by pressing something on a surface

metamorphic (meh • ta • MOR • fik) **rock** —rock that has been changed physically by heat, pressure, and water into a finer more compact form

paleontology (pail • ee • en • TAHL • oh • gee) —the study of fossils

petrified (PET • rih • fyed) —changed into stone

preserve (prih • ZERVE) —to save; to keep

rare (RAIR) —not found or seen very often; unusual

resin (REH • zin) —a sticky substance that comes from certain trees or other plants

scavenger (SCAV • en • jer) —an organism that feeds on dead matter

sedimentary (sed • ih • MEN • ter • ee) **rock** —a type of rock made from small pieces of matter that were once in water

silica (SILL • ih • kah) —a chemical found in some types of rocks

tissue (TIH • shoo) —a group of plant or animal cells that are alike

INDEX

About the Author

Allan Roberts received his undergraduate degree from Earlham College. As a participant in the National Science Foundation Academic Year Institute, he received his master's degree from the University of Georgia. Currently a biology teacher at Richmond High School in Richmond, Indiana, Allan has taught for more than twenty-three years. In addition to his regular classroom activities, he has taught at Indiana Extension University and special classes for the young. Many of his research articles and photographs have been published. His photographs also have appeared in the National Geographic, Reader's Digest, Audubon, National Wildlife *and many textbooks.*